THE VIETNAM PHOTO BOOK

The Vietnam Photo Book

Mark Jury

PREFACE BY BERNARD EDELMAN

VINTAGE BOOKS
A DIVISION OF RANDOM HOUSE
NEW YORK

FOR NINK

With thanks to the anthropological cinematographer,
hilarie's mother, my 1968D penny . . . and special
thanks to Cornell Capa for being Cornell Capa.

First Vintage Books Edition, September 1986
Copyright © 1971, 1986 by Mark Jury
Preface copyright © 1986 by Bernard Edelman

Library of Congress Cataloging-in-Publication Data

Jury, Mark.
  The Vietnam photo book.

  1. Vietnamese Conflict, 1961–1975—Pictorial works.
I. Title.
DS557.72.J87 1986 959.704'3'0222   86-40131
ISBN 0-394-74661-9

Manufactured in the United States of America

Preface

Mark Jury was sent to Vietnam in July 1969. This was not one of the military's wisest decisions.

Drafted into the Army, he was eager not to fight in the war but to document it. For the next twelve months, armed with a trio of bruised and battered Nikons (one would eventually be retrieved from where it had been dropped—the bear pit in the Saigon zoo) and supplied with thirty-six-exposure rolls of Tri-X by his aunt in Pennsylvania, Specialist 5 Jury roamed Vietnam more or less at will, unrestrained by rank. His assignment as an Army photographer was nebulous, and he took full advantage of his situation. Shooting film instead of ordnance, he captured the "quiet" war beyond the body count, the ambience of the fire bases and hospitals and offices. Mostly he caught the symbols and scrawls of peace and rebellion of a new generation of soldier less enamored with winning than with simply surviving his tour in the whacked-out war.

These images, of course, do not—cannot—mask the toll of combat: the maimed bodies and tortured psyches, the mutilated countryside, the uprooted refugees. And the dead. By 1969 more than thirty-five thousand Americans—and how many Vietnamese?—had been killed in the war without end; twenty thousand more—and how many Vietnamese?—would die before America would finally extricate herself from the quagmire. If anything, the photographs of the "other" war make the losses of the TV war that much more telling.

When Mark arrived in country—he was assigned to USARV-IO, one of the largest and possibly most irrelevant information offices in the Army—the character and tenor of the war were changing. The continuing pursuit of victory, so elusive and ultimately unachievable despite the reams of glowing statistics promulgated by the Pentagon, was taking on new, politically expedient guises: "pacification," the herding of peasants from "villes" in the unsecured countryside into "safe," controllable hamlets; and "Vietnamization," the shifting of the burden of combat from American troops back to the Vietnamese.

At the same time, antiwar demonstrations of increasing frequency and fervor, fueled by the revelations of the massacre at My Lai, were becoming part of the political landscape on the home front. Richard Nixon, who had inherited the war from a beleaguered Lyndon Johnson, began the phased withdrawal of American troops, whose number had peaked at 543,400 in March 1969. President Nixon also initiated the Paris peace talks. While ultimately successful, these negotiations were greeted in the field by skepticism bordering on disbelief as both sides postured for months over the shape of the table at which the talks were to be held.

Out in the boonies—in the triple canopy jungle of Vietnam and Cambodia and Laos, in the rice paddies from the Mekong Delta to the DMZ—the nasty little war of fire fights and booby traps, night ambushes and search and destroy missions continued. There were few major encounters, no brilliant strategic thrusts. And despite the My Lais of the war and the bad raps with which returning troops were greeted, they fought well, and they fought bravely.

But, in increasing numbers, their hearts weren't in the fight. The ferment back home in "the World" and the realities of their narrow slice of the war were changing them. Many smoked dope—marijuana, cheap and abundant, could even be purchased rolled, filtered, and sealed in packs of Winstons and Park Lanes. Some sampled, with disastrous results, smack—94 to 98 percent pure heroin ferried in, everyone knew, by Vietnamese generals via the CIA-chartered Air America. There were more and more reports of soldiers fragging their officers and refusing to seek contact with the enemy. The so-called credibility gap—the difference between what was and what the government was saying—seemed only to burgeon, magnified by news media increasingly dubious of pronouncements from the Pentagon or the president. The rationale for the American presence—we were there to "save" Vietnam from communism, to halt the spread of communism at Qui Nhon instead of Kansas City, etc., etc.—was wearing thin. "Our" Vietnamese, it appeared, were being led by the corrupt and the incompetent, just as those running the show for the United States were proving to be neither the best nor the brightest. And our Vietnamese, by and large, were simply no match for the North Vietnamese Army.

This was the war Mark Jury found, and filmed, in Vietnam. With the inquiring eye of the photographer and the sensibilities of the journalist, he explored the consequences of combat, the contradictions, the absurdities of the war. His photographs and anecdotes tell more about what the war was about, perhaps, than most of the photo spreads in the newsweeklies and the three-minute stories on the nightly news that ran at the time.

I met Mark in April 1970, when I was assigned to his unit after arriving in Vietnam. Mark was the vet and I was the "cherry." He knew what was going on—by then he had been there nine months—and how to work the system. He wasn't wasting his time: he knew he was going to do a book, even if he might get blown away in the process.

As a broadcast specialist I was able to travel with Mark from our base at Long Binh to Saigon, to the 91st Evacuation Hospital in Chu Lai, to Cambodia during the incursion in May 1970. (It was in Cambodia, in some nameless patch of jungle, that Wiley Dean Hooks of Metter, Georgia, whom I was to replace, bought it. The Cobra gunship in which he was flying, photographing the war, crashed. Was he blown out of the sky by enemy fire? Did the pilot lose control of his craft while strafing the Viet Cong pinning down a friendly unit? Who knows. Wiley was listed as a "non-combat" casualty, a category conceived by the same people who came up with the body count as a measure of success on the battlefield—and a means of making American losses somewhat less unpalatable to the folks back home.)

On one jaunt into Cambodia, Mark and I spent a few days at a fire base called Brown. A week earlier, in the only sustained engagement of the incursion, fifty VC and a handful of GIs were left dead on the berm. While we were there, a few more grunts were killed on night patrols. And it rained. Brown, strategically situated on a dried-up lake bed, became a morass of mud and water. For hours we bailed out the TOC (Tactical Operations Command) with helmets. Then, in a sandbagged hooch, we sipped C-ration hot chocolate as a captain played Simon and Garfunkel's "Sounds of Silence" and Pete Seeger's "Where

Have All the Flowers Gone?" on his guitar. The next day we photographed what would not quite have made it into *Time* or *Newsweek*: portraits of grunts grateful for the respite from forays into the bush.

A few weeks later—or was it before?—we spent a few hours at Phu Bai, up north, on the way to somewhere else, with a black sergeant, eighteen and a half years in the service, who had been relegated to composing commendations. It seems that his wife back in San Francisco was participating in antiwar protests, to the chagrin of the authorities on the post where she lived. The sergeant, a decent man, was weary. And appalled. He had just written up a citation for a general and his sergeant major. They had arrived at an obscure fire support base the morning after the NVA had attempted to overrun the outpost. Hovering in their chopper, they shot at the dead bodies along the perimeter. For their heroic actions at rallying the troops they recommended each other for medals: a Silver Star for the general, a bronze for the sergeant major.

This was the other war that rarely made it into the nightly news. This was the war that Mark Jury documented.

Mark left Vietnam in July, his tour completed. He had shot a couple hundred rolls of black-and-white film. He went home to his wife and a baby daughter eight months old—Hillary is almost seventeen now—and to work on what would become this book. It would be, in a sense, a yearbook of his time in Vietnam: photographic essays, buttressed by anecdotes, of what he had observed. There are no poignant depictions of battle, no scenes of carnage, no bloody corpses in grotesquely harmonious array. There are, rather, a remarkable assemblage of affecting images that illuminate the human costs of the war, photographs that complement the combat work of Larry Burrows and Eddie Adams, Philip Jones Griffiths and David Douglas Duncan.

When *The Vietnam Photo Book* was first published in 1971, it was one of the first books of any kind about the war in Vietnam. It quickly became a favorite with the men and women who had been there. It is republished now for them, and their children, for those too young to remember the details of the first televised war in history, for those who understand that a war is more than the sum of its battles. Mark Jury exposes some of the unsettling truths of the Vietnam War, the incongruities of life, and death, in the combat zone.

—BERNARD EDELMAN
New York City
26 April 1986

Introduction

In the late spring of 1968, there were nine U.S. Army induction notices pinned to the wall of my grandparents' home in northeastern Pennsylvania. Because I was a constantly moving magazine photographer, my aunt would give my *last* motel as my current address when the draft board called. The induction notice would show up at the motel and then be forwarded to Pennsylvania. Apparently, the game was getting old—an FBI man showed up at the house looking for me.

I had a dilemma: intellectually, I was repulsed by what was going on in Vietnam, but viscerally—in my gut—I was fascinated by what I felt was the over-powering experience of my generation. The "easy outs" available—a job deferment or a doctor's letter describing an ailment or crying "bed wetter"—held no appeal. I wanted to experience Vietnam; I didn't want to kill anyone.

My dilemma was resolved when I met an Army information officer to whom I described my ambivalent feelings about Vietnam and he said: "Do both." With my civilian experience, he explained, I should have no trouble being assigned to a special outfit—like *Stars and Stripes*—as a correspondent. The secret was to contact these outfits ahead of time. Once in Vietnam, I'd bypass the regular assignment process and go directly to the special outfit. By some sort of military hocus pocus, the outfit would then have new orders cut for me, disregarding whatever computer assignment my body may have received.

Armed with this knowledge, I "volunteered" for the draft. Ironically, I was sent to an Army base in Georgia and had to keep lobbying for Vietnam. Dee, my wife, was pregnant by then and benign company commanders kept suggesting I stay in the States.

However, my orders finally came through and I discovered the information officer was right. I chose the information office at U.S. Army Headquarters at Long Binh. In 1969, with the military and the news media hopelessly polarized, USARV-IO had become something of a dumping ground for those on the Army's "watch list"—the sons of rich and famous Americans who required special care while serving their country.

It was remarkable how it worked. When you have someone in the IO office at Army headquarters, for example, who's the son of a media titan and his mother is sending him care packages from the "21" Club in New York (personally delivered by a two-star general) and he's flying into Saigon for dinner with old family friend Ambassador Ellsworth Bunker, well, the brass really didn't have much interest in us common folk.

So, I split.

With my blanket travel orders and the Army's top press card, I spent the entire year roaming Vietnam and Cambodia at will. I traveled with three jackets: one had U.S. ARMY lettered on it, another USAID (United States Agency for International Development), and the third had the name of a major news-weekly. Depending on the situation, one of the shirts always guaranteed access.

Shortly after I arrived in country, a chance encounter took place that greatly affected my time and effort in Vietnam. A soldier in the press office at Chu Lai looked at my cameras and asked, "You a photographer?"

"Yeah," I replied.

"Some books came from Special Services today," he said. "One of them is about a photographer." He went over to a box of books and pulled out a volume with a tan cover. It was *Images of War* by Robert Capa.

I had never heard of Capa. But this book! It opened new vistas. Words and pictures. The photographer as participant. Making judgments. Attempting to analyze and comment on experiences. For the next year I carried the book in my pack, each day photographing and writing down my experiences for the book that *I* would do.

The unlimited access gave me a constant overview of the wacko war being fought to a rock 'n' roll sound track. (On my first gunship sortie, I was stunned when the pilot flipped a switch and the strains of "Happiness Is a Warm Gun" flooded the earphones in my helmet as the Huey dove at a tree line with miniguns blasting.)

One day I would be at the command mess at Long Binh listening to the generals discuss the merits of the new chef's Baked Alaska and the next day I'd be out humping with the First Cav and someone would step on a land mine.

Increasingly, I returned to the 91st Evacuation Hospital. While most of the men in Vietnam at this time were more concerned with facing a hostile barmaid than facing hostile fire, soldiers were still being killed every day.

After the arrival of each group of medevaced casualties, some would go to intensive care or a ward. The dead would go into the body cooler to wait for Graves Registration. I'd look at the bodies in the cooler. Eighteen, perfect health, stomach like wash boards, with an actuarial life expectancy of decades. It was as if this great machine of government had gone through an enormous process to winnow out the most healthy specimens of its society. And then kill them. Absurd.

And the war that was winding down was still devastating the Vietnamese. I would travel to the Quaker Prosthetics Center at Quang Ngai, but even there I couldn't find absolution through a Nikon. A young boy, missing both legs, looked me squarely in the eye and said, "You no-good GI."

Back in the United States, I began assembling the book. Naïvely, myopically—even ludicrously—I was obsessed with the belief that if only people *knew* what was going on over there, a mighty change would take place.

However, the country was already beginning the decade-long drift of *denying* Vietnam. If the country didn't want to hear the message, it had no interest in the messenger—books about Vietnam were out, I was told by everyone. Consequently, I was very excited when Cornell Capa, *Life* photographer, writer, and editor, agreed to look at the material.

Dee and I showed up at Capa's New York apartment at eight in the morning. After incessant knocking, a sleepy Cornell Capa—dressed in a bathrobe—opened the door. He had returned from Mexico in the wee morning hours, just as we were leaving home.

When Capa and Edie, his wife, learned that we had come all the way from Pennsylvania, they invited us in and the story unfolded. I had spoken with Cornell's secretary, a very precise woman, who told me that Capa would return at 8:00 A.M. on this date. She told me this so that I could make an appointment with him. I thought she was *making* the appointment!

No matter. We're there. Edie produced orange juice and cereal. Cornell began looking at the photographs. "There is something here I haven't seen" was his comment. He commanded me to return home and put the material into ten chapters and come back in a week so we could find a publisher.

A week later Cornell accompanied me to Grossman Publishers. They weren't keen about a book on Vietnam and had only agreed to look at the dummy as a personal favor to Cornell. Dick Grossman began looking through the images and skimming the text and said decisively, "We'll do it." *The Vietnam Photo Book* was published in 1971, excerpted in the last issue of *Look* magazine, used in a documentary by NBC, and reviewed in hundreds of newspapers.

It didn't stop the war.

In the fifteen years since the book was first published, America has endured a continuing catharsis over Vietnam. After a media-induced decade of stereotyping all vets as drug-crazed baby killers, there's now a sense that Vietnam veterans are not pariahs— a sense of understanding and even acceptance. It's one factor, along with time, that has enabled many vets to get the demons—if not behind them—at least under control.

In the numerous inquiries we received requesting that we reprint *The Vietnam Photo Book*, an underlying sense seemed to be that now the vet, and the non-vet, wanted a record of that time, as something to reflect upon. In 1971 we were all simply *too close.*

Ironically, as the country has come to accept the Vietnam veteran, another phenomenon has emerged: a new generation regards the Vietnam veteran as a folk hero at best, a Rambo at worst. My daughter, Hillary, who was born when I was in Vietnam, and her friends are fascinated by the era. (They're also, God forbid, fascinated by Rambo.) I hope *The Vietnam Photo Book* is something to throw into the balance.

How do I feel about the photographs today? That's what I've been thinking about. Which has caused me to recall the last time I asked myself this question.

It was during the time I was coming to personal grips with Vietnam. Out of all the anger and rage and frustration I felt, I wanted to find something—one thing—positive about the whole mess. Something about the human spirit.

I thought about Dui, the little girl in this book who had lost both legs and one arm to a mine. How she struggled in grotesque pain, learning to walk on plastic limbs.

I decided to track her down, to find out what had happened to her. She must have survived. She had the spirit and the drive.

Finally, I learned what had happened to Dui: when it was time for them to leave Vietnam, the Quakers had to decide whether to take her to the States for adoption or return her to her family in a remote village. After great debate, they opted for her family.

However, the subsistence-level family was simply unable to care for her. It was too much—moving her around, helping strap on the plastic arms and legs. Finally, they left her outside the village, where she died.

When I look over the photographs from Vietnam now, I'm grateful for the healing that's taken place and that *The Vietnam Photo Book* is now "an old yearbook" for many. I'm also pleased that a whole new generation will have the opportunity to learn about the "real" war in Vietnam.

But when I look at the photographs of Dui, I still feel very, very angry.

—Mark Jury
Waverly, Pennsylvania
Memorial Day, 1986

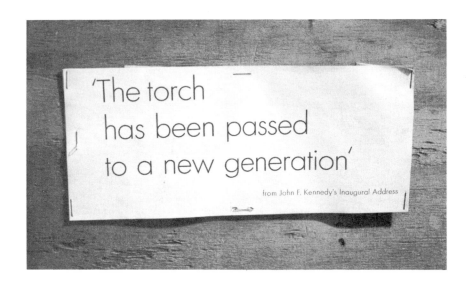

The New Action Army

"The New Action Army," boasts the recruiting posters. And it is. Caught by the draft (while all their friends were finding ways out) or intimidated by the draft into enlisting, they marched off unwillingly to an unwanted war. After the spring of 1967, the ranks were swelled by more college graduates than the Army had ever known. "General Hershey's Generation" was moved from the college campuses to Vietnam. And nothing in their background had taught them that protest doesn't pay.

The appearance of The New Action Army bewilders the "old Army" adherents. A new commander, seeing one of his line units return from the field, blurted out, "My God, they look like a band of hippies!"

"I don't care if they look like Tiny Tim and act like him," said another officer, "as long as they fight good."

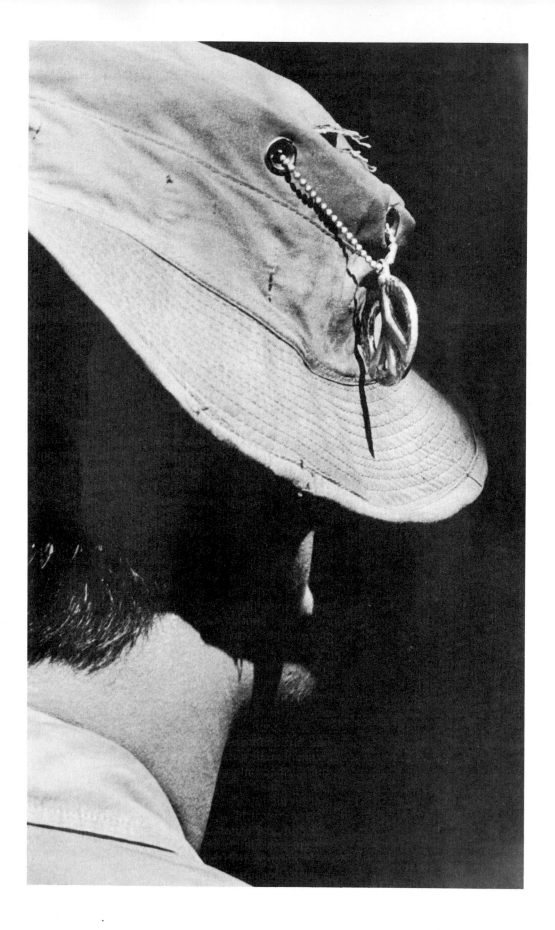

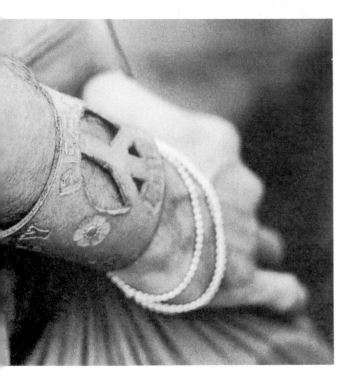

After I had been in Vietnam a while, I became bewildered at how the country's leaders could be so consistently wrong in reading the mood of the the young Americans who were forced to fight their war. When President and Mrs. Nixon visited Vietnam, I learned a lot.

Weeks before the Presidential party arrived, dozens of wounded GIs were interviewed. They were asked about their background, how they felt about being wounded, and how they felt about the war in Vietnam. Then they isolated in one ward the kids whose replies they knew would be "favorable." When Pat Nixon visited the hospital, it went something like, "Well, ma'am, these fellows will sure be glad you took the time to visit them. Here, let's go into this ward."

And the wife of the U. S. President walked up and down the aisles, talking with the wounded GIs.

"Yes, ma'am, I was riding on a truck that was hit with an RPG. Well, I don't know if I'll be able to use my arm again, but the doctors tell me once I get back to the States . . . you see, ma'am, I got two little brothers, ma'am, and I'd rather me fight the communists here than have my brothers hafta fight them at home."

And I'm sure that afternoon on Air Force One Pat Nixon honestly thought she was telling the President how the wounded kids felt about the war in Vietnam.

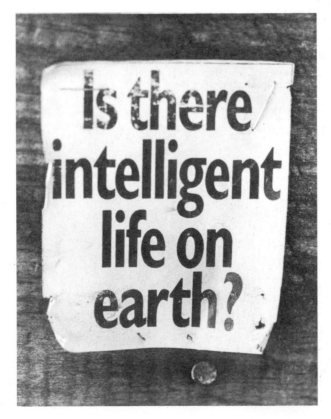

Count certain generals in the 10 per cent that normally fail to get the word. Some apparently haven't caught on to the fact yet that the World War II Churchill "V for Victory" sign is being used by antiwar groups as a peace symbol. In one news report quoting the two-star general involved, the post commander admitted he had been exchanging the peace sign with soldiers for three months before learning its current meaning.

"Washington News Briefs,"
Army Times, February 18, 1970

The fact that they wear love beads and peace medallions doesn't mean they can't fight. The kids learn quickly that the best way to stay alive is to kill the guy trying to kill you. And in combat they're ferocious. But once the fire fight is over, it's back to being peace and pot lovers. Often their opposition to the military has nothing to do with the moral aspects of Vietnam. It's just that they pick up a battered copy of *Life* Magazine and see everybody else skinny-dipping at Woodstock, and that's a hell of a lot better than "greasing gooks," fighting malaria, and maybe going home in a plastic bag.

These kids were part of a First Air Cavalry unit that had been "going on long, hot walks in the sun" in Vietnam. Month after month they didn't make contact, and after a while only a handful in the company had had any combat experience—a situation that gave the brass the jitters. Then, Cambodia broke; they were combat assaulted near a cache site and met enemy resistance. Even though their captain was wounded and medevac-ed out and they were taking casualties, the kids fought well and soundly trounced the NVA.

As soon as the dead NVA were buried, the company split into two groups—the "heads" and the

"juicers." Cokes were passed around, hard rock cassettes blared out of the small recorders, the discussion went back to the "fucking lifers," the "fucking war," and what was happening back in the States.

After a couple of days relaxing while securing the cache site, word came that a general from Saigon was coming out to inspect the captured goodies. Scissors, clean uniforms, razors, and shaving cream arrived with orders "to present a proper military appearance." The kids pitched the scissors and razors and used the shaving cream to ring the trees around the landing zone with peace signs.

When the general had finished looking over the booty, he stood on the helicopter skid and made a speech about what an outstanding job they all had done, ending with, "And gentlemen, I promise you what President Nixon said the other day. We will leave here as soon as our mission is accomplished."

From the back of the group came the voice of a very stoned GI: "Man, I don't ever want to leave this place."

THOUGHT FOR THE DAY: *The search for the best is a constant challenge to high adventure.—Selected U.S. Army Vietnam Daily Bulletin, April 3, 1970*

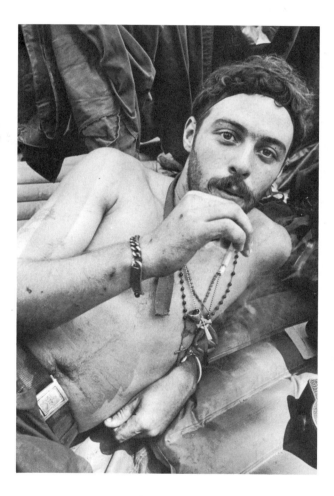

This kid showed me the belt buckle he had taken off an NVA officer killed in the fire fight while they were trying to take the cache site. Then he proudly showed me his tattoo.

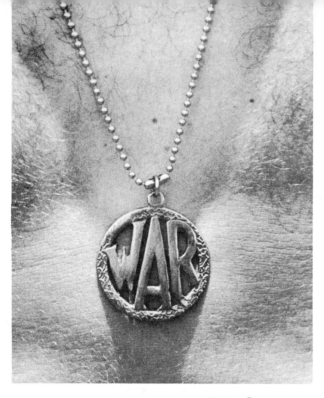

The peace symbol emblem was worn by thousands of young soldiers in Vietnam. Then a "war" medallion came on the market.

One old soldier noticed two shirtless kids—one with a peace medallion and one wearing a war emblem. "My God," he said, "who ever heard of people taking sides when they're supposed to be fighting a war?"

Two orderlies carried the wounded VC off the medevac and disappeared inside the hospital. A few minutes later one of the orderlies came out and handed me a calling card. "You want a souvenir?" he said. "This was stuck in the bandages. We get them all the time." He looked at the "dealers of death" card and mused, "Ummm, First of the Sixth. They've been kicking ass."

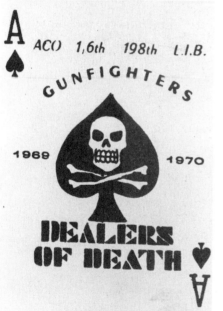

A
♠
ACO 1,6th 198th L.I.B.
GUNFIGHTERS

1969   1970

DEALERS
OF DEATH
♠
A

Those who kill for pleasure
Are sadists
Those who kill for money
Are professionals
Those who kill for both are
Gunslingers

LIVE BY LUCK
LOVE BY NATURE   KILL BY PROFESSION

DEATH ON CALL
WIRE Griffin SAN FRANCISCO 96383
C Btry 4th Bn (ARA) 77th Arty

INTRODUCING "THE KINGSMEN" U.S. ARMY
Assault Helicopter Company

SPECIALTIES: SIDE LINES:
Combat Assaults (Day &   Worlds Greatest Pilot
    Night)   International Playboy
LRRP, Ins. & EXTR   War Monger
Emergency Ammo Resupply   Renowned Booze Hound
Flareship & Phyops   Social Lion
Emergency Medivacs   Ladies Man
VC, Extermination
People Sniffer & Defoliation
PROVIDING: Death and Destruction 24-Hrs. a Day. If
           You Care Enough To Send The Very Best,
           Send KINGSMEN

The war in Vietnam is fought to a soundtrack of hard rock music. Twenty-four hours a day, 50,000 watts of clear channel broadcasting power take the latest sounds to 99 per cent of the U.S. troops in Vietnam. The source is the Armed Forces Vietnam Network—AFVN—which consists of six combination AM-FM radio stations (two FM stereo) and eight television stations.

The soundtrack adds a bizarre touch to the war. While tracks of the Eleventh Armored Cavalry swept through Cambodia, the Beatles were singing "Let It Be." During a fire mission at an artillery base, Steppenwolf's anti-war "Monster" blared through the din.

One afternoon I was photographing a group of grunts stringing claymore mines around a bleak hill near the DMZ. The only sound was a stream of rock coming out of a muddy, battered transistor radio. All at once I was aware of the words, telling of a young man who went to a war not of his choosing and returned to spend the rest of his life in a wheelchair.

"My God!" I said, "they're playing 'Ruby, Don't Take Your Love to Town.' "

One of the kids looked at me and grinned, "Yeah, they play it all the time."

The programming on AFVN bamboozles the military establishment. Specialist Four Kevin Kelly's rock music concert tours and a nightly underground radio show were based on the marijuana cult. The meaning of his performances went over the head of General Creighton Abrams, who sent Kelly two letters of commendation for raising troop morale.

Armed Forces Vietnam Network

Sgt. Pepper's Free Radio Program

. . . oh, heavy music, real heavy music (whistle). Back again to talk on the Sgt. Pepper Free Radio Program, and what do you have to say?

I believe that we have really been getting into some heavy songs . . .

Right, by some of the lesser known groups.

Yeah, and all of them seem to be moving and running in desperation . . . (heh-heh). See what you can find, and if you get there, call me and I'll come . . .

(Laughter . . .)

I can't think of anything else to say, so let's play some more.

(Military commercial on keeping shot record up-to-date)

Wow . . . that wasn't really in keeping with what wo've boon playing.

Uh, well now . . . (laughter). Edit! Speak, my friend. I was just wondering whether the sky was falling in, or if we're falling into the sky with this music.

I don't know, but here's Vanilla Fudge . . . (music). Sgt. Pepper until 8:00 . . . you can taste it—'Make Love Free . . .'

(Heavy rock . . .)

It's free . . . it's free . . . coming . . . coming. . . . It's free—it's coming—(faster) it's free—it's coming, it's free—it's coming . . . it's (pause) coming . . . (sigh) it's coming . . . (moan) it's free . . . (whisper) it's coming. . . . What! You blew it.

Look . . . (mumble) you jump out and shoot back . . . we don't know what we're doing here, folks (laughter). This is Sgt. Pepper . . . and Pistol Pete is eating crackers. And it's time to move on. . . .

(Military commercial on choosing Manila as a Rest & Recuperation site)

And here we are. This ends our space adventure for this evening . . . and where we went, we might not find out. Almost the whole program. And where we've been, we won't tell if you won't (laughter).

(Music)

We'll see you next week at this same time. Until then—give peace a chance.

24

Black Americans became increasingly bitter over their role in Vietnam as more and more brothers were drafted and sent to Southeast Asia. The idea of waging war on the Vietnamese people didn't sit well with them, and they knew that if they did live through their year in 'Nam, they still had to fight for their own freedom when they returned to the States. The military ignored the resentment until the infamous Long Binh stockade revolt, in which the brothers took over part of the stockade and GIs were killed and wounded in the melee. Then there was an incident at Da Nang's China Beach that almost resulted in a shoot-out with automatic weapons.

Overnight, the military started to get with it. Afros were "in" from then on, as were Black Power bracelets, short-timer sticks with a clenched fist, and more soul music in the clubs. But the brothers still stayed by themselves and were just as bitter about fighting a "white man's war."

The most common "Black is Beautiful" display, after the Afro haircut, was the "dap"—an intricate exercise of hand slapping, shaking, and gripping done by two brothers or sympathetic whites when they met. The military said, "The dap is O.K." and enterprising brothers expanded it to a loud, attention-getting performance. For many of the "old Army" sergeants, black as well as white, watching the black Americans go through their rituals was devastating.

It's not a war—
It's a happening

Black Power, peace signs, hash pipes, the radio playing "And When I Die" enroute to a combat assault. It was weird. One day as I left the office, another photographer was going through his repertoire of barks for his part as Snoopy in the play "You're a Good Man, Charlie Brown." On the plane to Da Nang an all-girl rock band from Detroit disconcerted everyone in their low-cut micro-miniskirts. And when I got off the plane an armored personnel carrier roared past the soft ice cream stand. In the forward hatch was a gorgeous blonde, her long hair blowing. "This isn't a war," I thought, "it's a happening!"

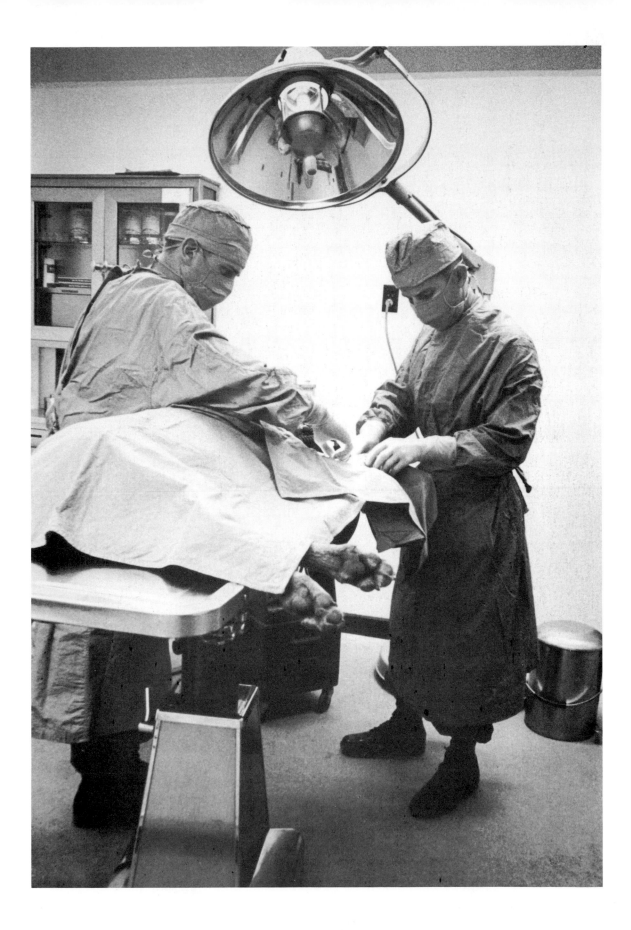

The crew of this artillery piece painted the name "Kiss of Death" on it. When a defective shell blew up in the chamber, one of the gunners was killed and two were seriously wounded.

Dr. Norman Vincent Peale, minister and author of *The Power of Positive Thinking,* always came on strong. In a hospital ward he arrived at the bedside of one young soldier who had just been awakened. He thrust his hand out to the groggy trooper with a booming, "Hello there, I'm Dr. Norman Vincent Peale from New York."

The trooper replied, "Glad to meet you, sir, but I'm happy with the doctor I have now."

"Fragging" is an institution in Vietnam. If the lifers make life unbearable, the kids will warn him with a CS (tear gas) grenade. If he persists, they'll "frag" him with a real (fragmentation) grenade. Unfortunately, the lifers aren't the only ones who suffer. Two lieutenants who had been in Vietnam only a few days were in this hootch when it was fragged. (This is the floorboard. Between the floor and where the grenade went off were the lieutenants.) The target—the lifer first sergeant—escaped injury.

In the field there're no problems. If and when a lifer is assigned to a combat company, he's put in shape quickly; the kids have the option to simply kill him during a fire fight. One unit's new first sergeant arrived when they were pulling "palace guard"—security for a headquarters. Usually it's a time for relaxation, but this guy was playing lifer, threatening punishment over "unmilitary appearance" and dope smoking. The first day

back in the field, one of the kids, a 6 foot 3 inch giant with long hair and peace symbols, said, "Watch this."

He walked over to where the lifer was, carrying an AK-47 (the NVA automatic rifle), and said loudly, "Yeah, I'm gonna take my old AK with me tomorrow 'cause I think we're gonna make contact." Then he spun around and looked down at the sergeant, straight into his eyes, and slowly brought the barrel of the AK up and said, "Sarge, if we make contact tomorrow, you better be real careful 'cause the new guys are the ones that get scared and do stupid things and get themselves killed. And, Sarge, those AKs do one helluva job on you."

The next time out with that unit, I learned that the sergeant had become a helluva good guy until he couldn't take it any more and was shipped back to the States.

Caught the midnight courier chopper from Saigon to Long Binh. Leaving the U.S. Army Vietnam headquarter complex when security guard says, "Hey, you guys photographers? You go around 'Nam taking flicks?"

We say yes, and he goes on. "Wow! You should see some of the flicks I got. Really outasight. Dead gooks and people blowed away. Shit, they're down at the hooch."

He wants to talk. Pulling guard alone all night around the same dark buildings gets pretty boring.

We ask the obvious "You spend some time in the field?" (It is obvious because the kids pulling security guard at Army headquarters must have a Combat Infantryman's Badge and a Purple Heart to qualify for the job.)

"Yeah," he says, "I spent twelve months in the field and got three Purple Hearts."

"What unit?"

He rattles off a string of fifth of this and seventh of that and vaguely I make out that he was with the Twenty-fifth Infantry Division operating around the Cambodian border—near Black Virgin Mountain.

We learn he was part of a sniper team that operated independently for the first part of his tour. He talks in a funny present tense, speaking about Smitty and Coons like we all know one another.

"What were you supposed to do?" I ask. "It sounds like you were just sorta wandering about on your own. Didn't you have any objective or anything?"

"The body count, man, the body count. All they wanted from us was a body count and we really gave 'em one. Shit, we'd do anything. And if you could bring in the body, they'd really go ape-shit. Wow, the old man [Commanding Officer] really ate that shit up. Or if you could bring in bloody clothes or an arm or a leg. Hell, once Smitty killed a baby pig and smeared the blood all over a gook's clothes and took it in to the old man. But he wouldn't buy that. Smitty was getting pretty uptight, though, because he'd been in country for two months and hadn't got a kill yet."

He tells us that finally they decided to hole up in an ARVN compound and call in their sitreps [situation reports] from there. And later they went into Saigon. The command finally found out and put them with a company.

He tells us about his wounds and shows us the scars from shrapnel on both his arms. The first two times he was wounded he was patched up at division headquarters and then rested at base camp until he was able to return to the field. Then he tells us about his last wound—an AK-47 round had gone through his helmet, ricocheted off his skull and went back out the top of his helmet.

"I was walking point," he said, "when the company made contact and I was trying to get back with the main part of the unit when—Blap! I felt myself get hit in the head and get blowed off my feet. Really, I got picked up off the ground and got blown back ten or fifteen feet and my head started hurting like hell and I thought, 'Oh Jesus, I've taken a round in the head,' and there was blood streaming down my face all over hell and then I passed out. I woke up about twenty minutes later, I guess, and my head felt so damn big and hurt like hell and I thought, 'Hell, I ain't dead,' and looked at the steel pot and there was two holes coming out of it and I thought, 'Damn, that round went out my helmet!' Ain't that a pisser."

We express our bewilderment and he goes on. "M. had a .51 cal round hit him right here (pointing to his right eyebrow), follow the bone around and just keep on going. Took off both his eyebrows."

He then tells us about an experience when he was a sniper. "Me and Smitty were sitting out in the tower all fucked up with the recorder playing and we see this door open down in the village and this VC come out. Well, there was a curfew and the mama-san knew that no one was supposed to be out. So I shot her right in the ass and the bullet just tumbled up through her body. Then this papa-san came out and Smitty shot him right through the head—a clean shot. Well, later we found out the old lady had come out to take a shit. So later there was this board of inquiry and Smitty and I walked in just smart-ass as hell and didn't salute this colonel or anything. Smitty just said, 'Waddyawant?' And the colonel asked us why we killed the gooks and Smitty told him, 'Shit, they were maybe VC and they weren't supposed to be out and who gave a fuck anyway, he'd killed dozens of gooks and all they ever wanted was the goddamn body count and nobody ever gave a shit who he'd killed before.' And the colonel said something and Smitty shouted back at him and told him he didn't know what the hell was going on and if he ever saw the fucking colonel out in the field he'd kill his ass and the colonel was white as hell and said, 'You will not talk to me like that, soldier.' Smitty was screaming and our old man was just eating that shit up. So the colonel slammed Smitty with insubordination and all this shit and busted him—I just stood there grinning—and hell, everybody forgot about us killing the two gooks."

I ask him what he plans to do when he gets out of the Army. "Just putt-putt around on my bike." (On convalescent leave in the States, he'd bought a motorcycle and attempted to ride from Sausalito to New York, but broke down in Denver.) I'll get $120 a month disability," he says, "and can sign up at some hokey junior college and get $175 and that's enough to putt-putt around on." He says he

has a few more months left before he gets out, but it isn't so bad because he can sort of pull guard whenever he wants. "Hell, if I don't feel like going on guard, I just pull out my profile. It says no walking, no prolonged standing, no running—hell, I can't do anything!"

I quickly calculate his time in the Army and say, "What'd you do, enlist for the field?"

"Hell no," he says. "I enlisted to be a telephone line repairman, but in basic they brought in the Golden Knight skydiving team and had a band and everything and I volunteered to go airborne. Hell, I didn't know you had to waive your enlisted MOS and become I 11B! Shit, I was just a seventeen-year-old punk kid anyway. Then when I came over here, I volunteered for sniper school."

He looks across the spacious grounds of the headquarters and says, "You know, out in the field you really live like animals, but at least you're a man. Here, I just couldn't take the harassment shit. . . ."

One morning in May the major ran into our office. His face was ashen and he was shaking. "Is your pack ready to go," he asked, "Can you catch a chopper in 15 minutes?"

"Yes," I answered, "why?"

"We're going into Cambodia," he said.

This was it! The war was back on. I had a pretty good idea that it was going to happen. My friends at the two Evac hospitals had called a few days before and told me that they were clearing out 600 beds. Preparing for an operation that expected 20% casualties. We were too far south for an invasion of North Vietnam. The other alternative was Cambodia.

I quickly made arrangements with another photographer for him to catch the chopper and I went over to the hospital. All afternoon, no casualties. Almost spooky. Everyone primed and then nothing. Early in the evening they began to trickle in. But the kids told of almost no resistance—it was as if the NVA had just vanished.

The next day I went into Cambodia and was greeted by some friends who were ebullient. They had stockpiles of beer, soda, ice, rations, stereo cassettes, everything. Where did it all come from? Trading . . . they were trading war souvenirs to helicopter pilots for all the goodies! One of the helicopter pilots said, "I've been in this damn place for 10½ months and haven't been able to get ahold of anything to take home. And these guys have it all right here. Hell, I'll fly into Saigon and bring a TuDo street whore house out here if they want it."

And the invasion of Cambodia became the Great Souvenir Hunt.

LIST OF NATIONS HAVING PROVIDED
AID TO THE REPUBLIC OF VIETNAM

ARGENTINA
AUSTRALIA
AUSTRIA
BELGIUM
BRAZIL
CANADA
REPUBLIC OF CHINA
COSTA RICA
DENMARK
ECUADOR
FRANCE
FEDERAL REPUBLIC OF GERMANY
GREECE
GUATEMALA
HONDURAS
INDIA
IRAN
IRELAND
ISRAEL
ITALY
JAPAN
REPUBLIC OF KOREA
LAOS
LIBERIA
LUXEMBOURG
MALAYSIA
MOROCCO
NETHERLANDS
NEW ZEALAND
NORWAY
PAKISTAN
PHILIPPINES
SINGAPORE
SOUTH AFRICA
SPAIN
SWEDEN
SWITZERLAND
THAILAND
TUNISIA
TURKEY
UNITED STATES OF AMERICA
UNITED KINGDOM
URUGUAY
VENEZUELA

47

That the Vietnam War resembles a happening doesn't change the fact that well over fifty thousand young Americans have died there, and thousands more will spend their lives staring at a ceiling wishing they had died there. And all the hullaballoo about the war "winding down" didn't help the kid in the field at all. In the fall of 1969, a typical grunt walked through the Americal Division headquarters at Chu Lai.

He sported long tousled blond hair with sideburns and a drooping mustache. Shirt open and towel around his neck. Hatless. Filthy jungle fatigue pants rolled up and mud-caked and cracked boots. He walked through the division base camp with his M-16 carried over his shoulder.

A major in starched fatigues and spit-shined boots approached the young soldier and began questioning him about his "unmilitary appearance." The soldier was aghast—he couldn't believe it.

The major smiled and said, "The war's over . . . we've got to start acting like garrison soldiers now."

The young soldier reached into his pocket and pulled out a grubby envelope and waved it at the major, "What do you mean the war's over?" he said. "Three months ago seven of us were at LZ Baldy and now five are dead!"

The major gave a sick smile, "Well, let's say it's slowed down quite a bit."

In Vietnam less than 15 per cent of the soldiers are doing the actual fighting and dying—and they're the ones who get the least from America. Safest are those young Americans whose family name has enabled them to be put on the Army's "Watch List," a document that keeps track of America's "elite" while they serve their country. The roster reads like a gossip column: cousin of a famous black movie star, relatives of powerful congressmen, sons of generals, neighbor of a high government official. Their assignments are carefully chosen and they can do no wrong.

At the other end of the spectrum are the disproportionate number of blacks, Mexicans, and sons of low-income Americans who become riflemen because they haven't any other skills. These are classified "underachievers" and taught how to be expert killers. Or the men to whom a judge has given a choice between prison or the infantry. And high school dropouts who enlist with dreams of learning electronics and then find their scores don't qualify them for the schools. So they become "11B"—the Army number for infantrymen—and spend their year killing and hoping they don't get hit.

Getting hit

I was in the emergency room of a large Army hospital when two orderlies rushed out with a litter. I followed them out to the medevac landing pad, and a few seconds later a helicopter with the familiar Red Cross painted on its nose touched down. I automatically raised the camera to my eye as they removed the casualty. Then, "My God!" Through the view finder I saw a GI with his pants cut away. A compress was over his testicles and blood was trailing down his leg onto the litter. And he was screaming in Spanish.

He was rushed into the emergency room along with a friend who had been wounded slightly when the grenade went off and spewed shrapnel. The kid was screaming in Spanish and bawling and his friend kept telling him to shut up.

Finally he stopped screaming and in English he moaned, "I knew this would happen when I came to 'Nam. . . . I didn't want to come to 'Nam. . . . I told my mother this would happen. . . . Oh God, I only got fifty-nine days left in the 'Nam. . . ."

Then he was wheeled into the operating room. "They'll probably have to castrate," said a doctor.

Outside I saw one of the Mexican-American orderlies I knew and asked him what the kid had been screaming in Spanish.

The kid answered, "He said they told him if he didn't come to Vietnam and fight, they would send him back to Puerto Rico for good."

"Their age and intellectual background have such great bearing on their outlook. You bring a nineteen-year-old kid in here who's just had his leg blown off above the knee and lost an arm and he'll say, 'Man, am I glad I'm alive!' And starts talking about how they can put on an artificial arm and leg and what kind of car he's going to get with modified controls.

"But when a young lieutenant, whose parents have just spent $12,000 to $15,000 to put him through college, is brought in missing limbs, he realizes what it's like to go through our society as a cripple. And many times, he'll usually lapse into depression. In fact, many times their mental state seriously hampers dealing with their physical needs. They just want to die."

An orthopedic surgeon at the Ninety-first Evacuation Hospital in Chu Lai, commenting on the increasing number of GIs losing limbs from mines and booby traps

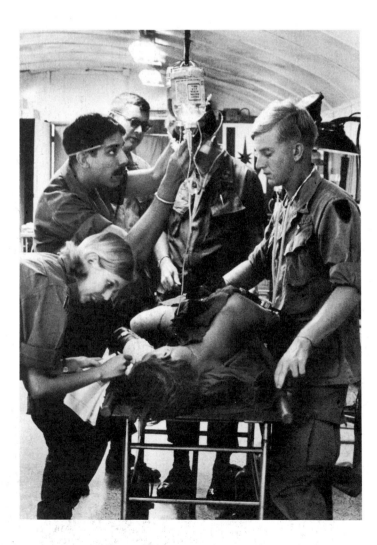

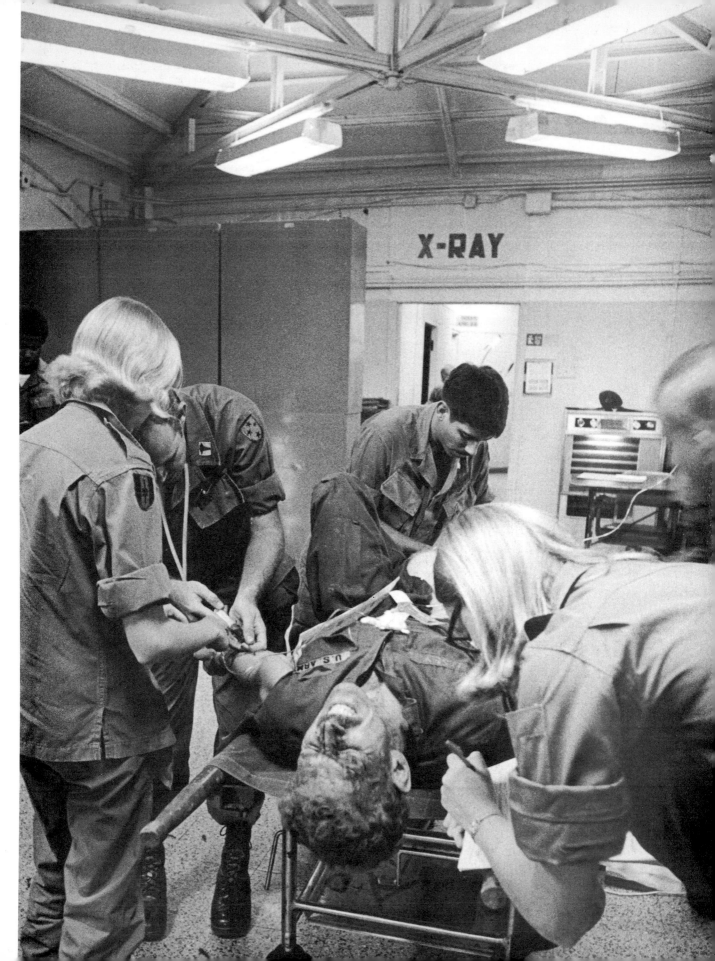

One of the Army recruiting posters features a scene of a fisherman on a placid lake, framed through the spreading branches of a tree. The caption reads, "Come home to your spot." It means that if a soldier re-enlists, he's guaranteed so many months' duty at a base near his home. At the A & D (Admission and Dispositions) section, the kids put up these posters in the cooler, where the bodies are kept until picked up by Graves Registration.

A KIA (Killed In Action) with a leg blown off is taken off the medevac chopper. He's a chartreuse-green color. They take him through the admitting room (past GIs on sick call) and out back, next to the cooler where the bodies are kept until positively identified, and then to Graves Registration. A fellow who works in A & D says this is one of five dead GIs that will be coming in. They were on a track that hit a mine.

Four kids from battalion headquarters arrive to identify the bodies and collect the valuables. It's a sick Russian roulette, because the kids from headquarters know that five men from their company have been killed, but they don't know who until the blanket is pulled back.

A kid from battalion goes back to the cooler to check the first KIA. A few second later he opens the door and calls out: "It was M._____"

One kid smashes his fist against the wall.

Another kid says, "Did you know him?"

"Did I know him," and with ice-cold eyes he just stares straight ahead. Silence.

The kid comes out and says, "He had $900 in his wallet."

"Yeah, he was going on R & R in a couple of days."

And speculation begins on whether or not his young wife may already be in Hawaii.

The kid had been given the job of cutting wedding rings off the fingers of dead soldiers. He had a small device with a blade and a screw that cut through a ring with little effort.

He wanted to demonstrate how the device worked, so we went back to the cooler where the bodies were. He put the blade over the ring and started twisting the screw to exert pressure. Instead of the band popping, the entire finger fell off. The body was that of a pilot whose helicopter had crashed in the Bien Hoa River, and it had been some time before the divers could retrieve the body.

The kid cursed and moved to a fresh combat killed-in-action body. He took the corpse's ring finger and jerked on it a few times before installing the device.

"IN WAR, WHEN A COMMANDER BECOMES SO BEREFT OF REASON AND PERSPECTIVE THAT HE FAILS TO UNDERSTAND THE DEPENDENCE OF ARMS ON DIVINE GUIDANCE, HE NO LONGER DESERVES VICTORY"

DOUGLAS MACARTHUR

The Paper Clip War

For the majority of young Americans in Vietnam, the possibility of getting hit doesn't even exist. They're stationed in "the Rear," busily engaged in the Paper Clip War. Well-fed, well-tanned GIs type out the millions of pieces of paper that sustain the American war machine, and engage in a thousand other support activities—from slot machine repair to volleyball instruction. For them the killing and dying war is just something they read about in *Stars and Stripes.*

The enemy at the Rear is the petty harassment of an organization with little to do and too many people to do it. Military haircuts, daily shave, starched fatigues, and shined boots are a must. But for those who can play the game, the time passes quickly at the swimming pool, club, sports events, movies, and endless parties.

A typical day at Army headquarters: a draftee with a college degree listens to Simon and Garfunkel as he types the endless stream of paperwork. The colonel's driver grapples with his latest hot rod model. And the sergeant major, who's earning over $10,000 a year from the U.S. taxpapers, pushes on with his all-consuming project—reading through the Encyclopedia Britannica.

"Anybody who spends twelve months over here deserves something . . . uh . . . and these two young men have done an outstanding job keeping the paperwork straight . . . up here."
Bronze Star presentation, September 7, 1969, Long Binh

The colonel comes into the office where a photographer is waiting to shoot the award ceremony.

Colonel: "Who's the award for today?"

Deputy: "T."

Colonel: "Him? He's the one with the rather unusual mustache."

Deputy: "He's the kind of guy who in a quiet way really gets to you. He's getting out of the Army—he doesn't even belong here."

Time for the ceremony. Everybody in the section files into the room. A rather disheveled kid comes in and stands next to the colonel. The captain begins reading the standard Bronze Star for Meritorious Service citation. The kid breaks into a grin. The captain reads on. The kid starts to snicker. The colonel's eyes widen, nostrils flare, he is breathing hard. Nervous virbrations throughout the room. The captain cuts the citation short. All of a sudden the colonel seems to realize he's a *colonel* in United States Army. He returns to military bearing, takes the Bronze Star medal and turns to the kid smiling. "Well, Specialist T., it gives me great pleasure. . . ."

"I think that's one of the nice things about this war. We get the woman's viewpoint from time to time. And it doesn't hurt any of us."
    Colonel awarding Bronze Star for Meritorious Service to WAC Sergeant First Class, March 27, 1970, Hq USARV, Long Binh

*"You know how they could end this war in a matter
of months? Just turn off the air conditioners. You
turn off the air conditioners and the colonels and
generals couldn't wait to get out of here."
Overheard in the spacious U.S. Army Vietnam
headquarters, Long Binh*

A GI and a WAC spend off-duty time as actors in a Special Services play at U. S. Army Headquarters, Long Binh.

"O.K., this time we don't want people up on the stage like they were last time and we don't want people throwing underpants and shirts on the stage like they did last time. So just stay off the stage and enjoy yourselves. Oh, one other thing. About the flares. We all know that the flares each have a meaning . . . uh, a red flare means a ground attack. So this time let's all leave the flares alone. Last time I spent an hour on the phone trying to straighten this out."

Commanding Officer, General Staff Company, U. S. Army Vietnam Special Troops before the stripper came on at a Company party

For officers, life at the Rear can be opulent. The command mess for generals and selected colonels at Long Binh is an ultraplush restaurant with an ample bar that could rival many first-class nightspots in the States. The service certainly exceeds that anywhere in the States. Vietnamese girls in traditional dress are waitresses, and enlisted men in white shirts and ties serve as bartenders and bus boys—keeping the glasses full of wine and passing out cigars on a silver platter after dinner. One kid who worked at the command mess as a bus boy had a degree in hotel management from Cornell; that's how he ended up pouring wine for generals.

One senior sergeant spent his time between Long Binh and Saigon making sure there was an ample supply of steak, lobster, and booze. Meals are sumptuous and there are always more meals than needed in case a stray general drops in.

We give one guy photographs of his dog; he gives us meals.

A typical meal:
Veal steaks stuffed with egg and spices
Baked stuffed potatoes au gratin
Broccoli with cheese sauce
Fresh rolls
Baked Alaska for dessert

One day a friend was walking by the command mess and took a snapshot of the place. He was immediately collared by MPs who demanded his film, saying the building was a "restricted area." Telling about the incident, he said, "What really pisses me off about it is that it's my tax money that built that place."

*"I couldn't even picture a place like this . . . hell!
I'd heard about Long Binh and Vung Tau and Cam
Ranh, but I thought they were under somewhat the
same pressures we were. Here they [the generals
and colonels at the bar] care about whether or not
the PX has their brand of beer and why we can't
get a certain kind of booze; they don't give a damn
about ammo or whether or not the convoy got
through."*

*SFC in charge of the menu at the command
mess, December 11, 1969, waiting for Astronaut
Borman to arrive for luncheon hosted by
the Deputy Commanding General*

Astronaut Frank Borman signs autographs for the
generals at a Command Mess luncheon. A more
gala affair was the dinner party thrown for Miss
America and her entourage.

NO MISSION TOO DIFFICULT, NO SACRIFICE TOO GREAT, DUTY FIRST

Ellsworth Bunker, the U.S. Ambassador to Vietnam for years, was the honored speaker at the redeployment service for the First Infantry Division. The "Big Red One" had been one the first divisions in Vietnam and now that the President of the United States had decided it was "time to end the war," the colors of the First were going back to Fort Riley, Kansas. Ellsworth Bunker took his speech from a manila envelope, looked at it a few seconds, and then waited patiently for his turn to speak.

Remarks for 1st Division ceremony, April 3, 1970
I am happy to see on your attractive program the comment, "We worked ourselves out of a job." As President Nixon put it in his speech on Viet-Nam on November 3 of last year, ". . . the primary mission of our troops is to enable the South Vietnamese forces to assume full responsibility for the security of South Viet-Nam."

The fact that we are able to redeploy this great fighting Division shows that we are successfully accomplishing this.

You have written another brilliant chapter in the history of the Division and have made a great contribution toward our objective in Viet-Nam. This is to preserve the right of the Vietnamese people to live under a form of government of their own choosing. At the same time, you have contributed to another extremely important objective, that of preserving the credibility of American commitments under the UN and SEATO treaties to resist aggression. I believe the continued credibility of those commitments is fundamental to our position as a great power. It is also fundamental to the mainte-

nance of the stability necessary to prevent the outbreak of another world conflict.

The 1st Division has contributed to a great cause here which goes beyond the confines of Viet-Nam. It goes to the heart of the question of whether we as a nation have the patience and the will to accept the responsibilities of power. It goes to the heart of man's unending struggle for freedom and dignity.

As always in its distinguished history, it has met the test in a magnificent manner. I have known many of the officers and men of your Division personally, and I am proud of them and of all of you as Americans and as fighting men.

My congratulations and best wishes go with you. God bless you all.

Ellsworth Bunker

Following Ambassador Bunker's speech, my friend called the U.S. Embassy and talked with a secretary.

"What's the story on Bunker's speech," he asked, "about the credibility of the U.S. commitment in Southeast Asia and all that? It sounds like Johnson days. This is 1970—nobody buys that."

"Well, it was an old speech," she said.

"Doesn't he have any new speeches?"

"Ambassador Bunker has been ill," she replied.

74

Celebrities—
year-round invasion

Raquel Welch started questioning an institution when she returned from her 1967 Vietnam tour with Bob Hope.

"Sending girls like me to Vietnam to entertain the troops is like teasing a caged lion with a piece of raw meat," she said. "I'm not criticizing our boys' thoughts or feelings one bit, I'm just telling you that I know what is going through their minds. There they are, fighting an aimless war in a foreign land where they aren't wanted. . . . Deep down inside, I think it would be best if stars like me stayed home and the Government sent off troupes of prostitutes instead. After all, when you get right down to it, those boys want relief, not more frustration."

In 1969, during his first show, Bob Hope said, "Well, fellows, I've just talked with President Nixon . . ." and was booed. And everywhere he went there were peace signs and a strange smell in the air. The old trooper just didn't understand these new soldiers.

At each press conference, the reporters kept asking Bob Hope, much to his chagrin, why the kids had booed when he mentioned Nixon. They also asked him about the quote from a well-known sex symbol about how his show teased the men.

To that, Hope shot back, "We're all chipping in to buy that famous actress a brain."

And finally, they asked him about the members of his cast exchanging peace signs with the GIs.

Hope became a little flustered and retorted, "I don't get this 'peace' sign all the time. Winston Churchill used the 'V' sign, you'll remember. Anyway, I don't think any of the entertainers with me would do anything to hamper the effort over here."

While he was explaining, one of the young lovelies with him gave the "V" sign to one of the GI reporters and winked.

Fire Bases

The bulk of GIs who aren't grunts and aren't at the Rear spend their year on a fire support base. Hundreds of fire bases exist in Vietnam, enabling the U.S. to blanket almost every foot of the country with artillery fire.

At the fire bases, the GIs don't go through hell or face death like the grunts, and they're usually exempt from the petty harassment of the Rear. For them, the overriding problem is boredom. For one year they sit on a little hunk of dust or mud, cleaning their artillery pieces, reading, writing letters home, and waiting for the signal, "Fire mission!" at which they leap into action.

Under the boredom, however, is a pervading apprehension that their base might be fire-base-of-the-week-that's-overrun. Periodically one of the outposts comes under enemy attack, and although it is well fortified, often the NVA break through the perimeter and overrun the base.

Fire Support Base Fuller

Fire Support Base Fuller was the northernmost U. S. base in Vietnam. Overlooking the DMZ, it perched atop a pile of rocks, 1,800 feet high, and only thirty-five yards at the widest spot. Fuller was supplied only by air, and at times it was fogged in for a week or more, so the small group stationed there became a real family. Across from Fuller is another pile of rocks where the Marines had a well-publicized combat base known as "the Rock Pile." The Marines are gone now, and their bases have been abandoned—Dong Ha, Vandergrift, Con Thien, Khe Sanh. No heroics for the draftees left behind to man the artillery in support of the Vietnamese. All they want to do is put in a year and get on board their "freedom bird."

THOUGHT FOR THE DAY: *There are some defeats
more triumphant than victories.—Montaigne*
U.S. Army Vietnam Daily Bulletin,
March 27, 1970

The most exciting thing that had happened at
Fuller in months was the sick baby ocelot that
wandered into the base. The men were keeping it
in the communication shack, the warmest spot on
the base, and treating it with milk of magnesia and
pencillin shots.

The main activity is polishing and repolishing
brass shell casings for hours until they glisten
—then using them as souvenir ashtrays. Once a
month one of the GIs takes all the finished ashtrays
back to Dong Ha to get them engraved. This GI
put a "freedom bird" on his ashtray.

Fire Support Base J. J. Carroll

Fire Support Base J. J. Carroll isn't isolated like Fuller. At Carroll they have more room and a mess hall; they can drive by jeep to a larger base camp for PX runs and the nightly movie.

At Carroll the problem is the mud—acres of deep, sucking, wallowing mud. The strange thing is that walking in the mud is just like walking on ice. The problem isn't so much sticking as it is slipping and sliding. In fact, one of the major diversions of the place seems to be recounting stories about dramatic falls in the mud by unfortunate gunners.

There's an eight-inch self-propelled howitzer battery here—enormous guns with names painted on them: ANDY CAPP, FAT ALBERT, and ANGRY ANGEL. They hurl high explosive charges up to twenty miles away in support of ground units and as a defense on other fire base perimeters. The kids manning the guns have attended some sort of Army school and have quite a lot of pride in the guns, keeping them clean and working properly, and not complaining too much about carrying the eighty-pound shells into place.

As usual, I'm inundated with a barrage of questions: What's it like in Saigon? What's it like humping? The pattern is alway the same; they're trying to feel me out so that they can figure where isolated FSB J. J. Carroll fits on the scale. I'm vague in my answers, and things are just about the same in their minds as they were before I arrived—not as good as Saigon or Da Nang, but a helluvalot better than the plight of the grunts.

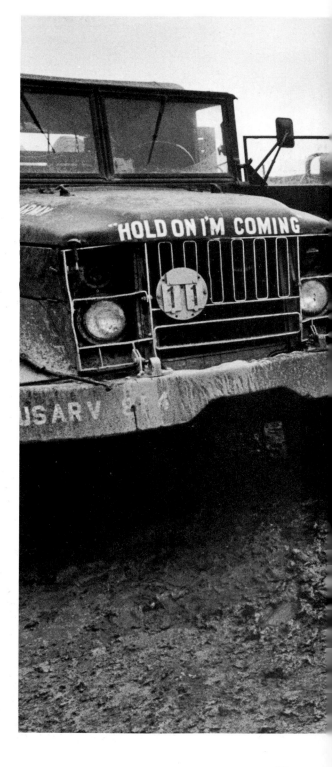

We were getting ready to board the jeep and leave
Fire Support Base J. J. Carroll.

A sergeant came up and said, "Bring back three
cases of dry."

"Dry what?"

"Dry anything," he said. "We'll scatter it about
and make people happy."

I went into the captain's room to thank him for
his hospitality. He wasn't there, but the book he
was reading was open on his desk. It was Bernard
Fall's *Hell in a Very Small Place.*

Far across the base, a kid noticed an outsider was aiming a telephoto lens in his direction. So he threw up both arms and communicated the only way he could.

95

Fire Support Base Wood

The kids at Fire Support Base Wood would love to see rain. They're choking in heavy black dust and one hundred-degree temperatures. Choppers bring in a steady stream of supplies and kick up even more dust. Wood has only been in existence a few days and there's much activity. Some of the kids at Wood were at another fire base that was overrun a few days earlier. The remnants were moved a short distance away, replacements arrived, and this piece of dirt is being resurrected as Fire Support Base Wood.

The command sent the First Cav band out to Wood to raise the morale of the troops. Hot chow, beer and soda, newspapers, and mail were also sent. But for those who remembered the hand-to-hand fighting in the dark and the Americans shooting at each other in the confusion, all the trimmings were unimportant.

We go over to a group just in from the field. One kid is talking about I., the soldier the overrun fire base was named after, who had been put in for the Silver Star a few days before he was killed.

"We were humping the boonies (patrolling) when the pointman got hit and he was laying out there wounded and we were trying to get to him but the fire was just too damn much. I. was next to me and he says 'Fuckit' just like that. He says 'Fuckit' and gets up and runs out—through this wall of fire—and picks up the pointman and comes back with him. That's why they put him in for the Silver Star. But a couple of days later the guy got hit with a B-40 round and he was messed up. God, was he in bad shape. But he had more guts than anyone I've ever seen and he kept trying to sit up and I was trying to hold him down and he kept saying, 'Hey, give me a drink of water,' and finally he got up and saw it was me and he said, 'Moore, you son of a bitch, why won't you give me a drink of water?' God, I never prayed before in my life, but I prayed 'Dear God, please don't let this man live,' because he was hit so bad he just would've been a vegetable."

I. died and the fire base was named after him. Shortly after, the first enemy mortar round hit the ammo dump and it was all downhill. The NVA broke through the perimeter. It was one of the worst beatings a single U.S. unit had taken in almost two years.

Winning hearts and minds

Groups of GIs wandered about the country to help the Vietnamese people, and win their support away from the Viet Cong. This was the highly touted "other war" of building roads, and hospitals, digging wells, and showing the people how to raise hogs. Once the military was committed to the effort, millions of dollars were dumped into it and hundreds of civil affairs companies jumped into action. At the same time, the Army public relations organization began cranking out millions of words of propaganda about "winning the hearts and minds of the people."

But soon the phrase became a big joke. One GI poster showed a hulking U.S. soldier talking with a Vietnamese couple. The caption: "Let Me Win Your Heart and Mind or I'll Burn Down Your Goddamn Hut." So the Army sent out word that GI writers were never again to use the phrase "winning hearts and minds." Instead they should use "develop community spirit or equivalent descriptive phrases."

Typical of the "other war" was an elaborate four-color publication that was given out to the Vietnamese, telling of the U.S. going to the moon. One old man sat morosely in the corner, refusing the offer of a copy.

On the way back to the base, a GI who could speak Vietnamese said, "Do you know what was wrong with that old man? His crops failed this year and when he learned that men were walking on the moon, he said now he knew why they had failed."

A couple of days after arriving in Vietnam, I went to a village to observe the civil affairs people in action. We met a lieutenant and a USAID civilian and began a tour of the village. Where shells had impacted, a house had been totally demolished, leaving only rubble. Supposedly, the Vietnamese had been given bricks to rebuild their homes, but they sold the bricks on the black market. The families were huddled in an alleyway. They didn't have food. The children were sick.

After looking at the former home sites, I said to the lieutenant, "I don't understand why these homes are just demolished at random. What do the Viet Cong do, shell indiscriminately?"

He turned and looked at me to make sure I wasn't putting him on, and then said, "They weren't enemy shells."

Three senior noncommissioned officers were part of an advisory team that was to "Help the Vietnamese Help Themselves." They were to supply the materials and advice for the men of the village to build a water tower that would supply running water.

For weeks the advisory team traveled to the village to show the men how to build a water tower, but the Vietnamese just weren't interested.

Back in Saigon, the major asked the NCOs how the project was coming. They told him the Vietnamese still wouldn't build the tower.

The major said, "Well, in a few weeks the colonel is going to tour the villages to see how well this program is working. And gentlemen, when the colonel gets to our village, there *will* be a water tower."

So the sergeants went back to the village and began building the water tower themselves. All the young men gathered around and laughed and joked while the old, out-of-shape soldiers struggled

and sweated with the sheets of steel. If one of the sergeants slipped or dropped his end, they would all laugh and clap.

Finally, one sergeant exploded and screamed at the crowd, "You fucking lazy gook bastards! You can't even hang on to your own country and all your wives and daughters are whores. I wish to hell I was in the field and could call air strikes in on your lazy fucking asses!"

As expected the colonel arrived at the village. He gave one medal to the major who had advised so splendidly on the project, and another medal to the village chief, for the fine work his people had done in actually building the water tower. After the colonel's visit, the advisory team did not go back to install the pump. The village never did get running water.

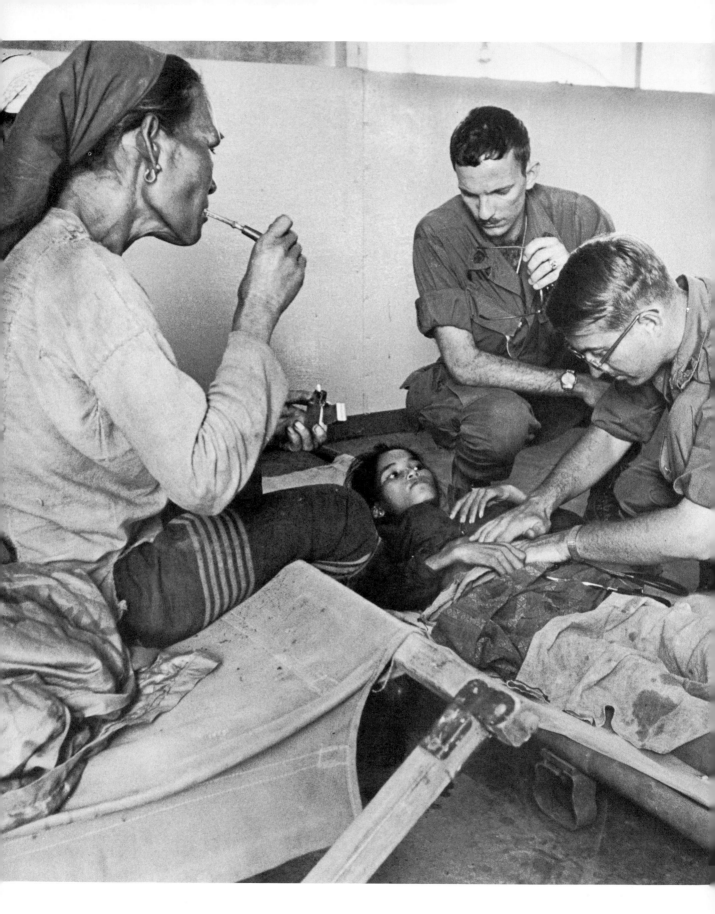

Some Americans managed to transcend the bureaucracy of "pacification" and actually help the Vietnamese caught up in this war. But it was always on the personal rather than official level. I met Kenneth R. Case, Jr., M.D., a captain in the U.S. Army, at an obscure Montagnard village.

His assistant Smitty was a young enlisted man who had been a divinity student, and once in the Army had become a medic. When he arrived in Vietnam his orders read 29th CA Company; when he asked what CA meant, they said "Combat Assault." So with visions of soldiers jumping out of helicopters with knives in their teeth, he reported to the Twenty-ninth *Civil Affairs* Company where he met Dr. Case. Together they traveled about Vietnam doing what good they could. Smitty learned to speak Vietnamese fluently, developed a real love for the people, and extended in Vietnam three times until his Army enlistment was through.

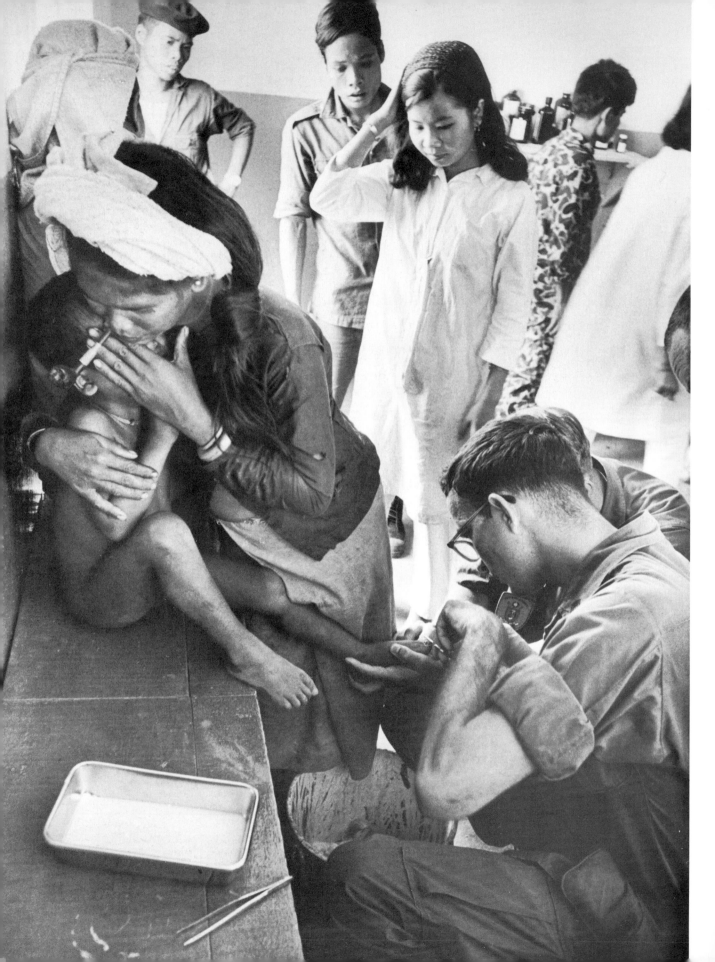

"Dr. Case, what are the qualities needed for civil affairs work?"

"Well, the person has to be a mature individual. He has to be able to recognize the situation we're in—all the politics, the bad government, the unjust war—and in spite of this, he's got to be able to accept all this and still have a desire to do something for people because they're people. Not because they're "gooks" or because his government puts him in the job and says he will. This is kind of easy for a doctor, because this is what he devotes his life to anyway. The fact that they happen to be Vietnamese people doesn't really make too much difference."

"The U.S. Army Vietnam uses us in various civic action programs to sooth our conscience for the damage we're doing to this country."

Dr. Kenneth R. Case, Jr., Public Health Officer,
Twenty-ninth Civil Affairs Company

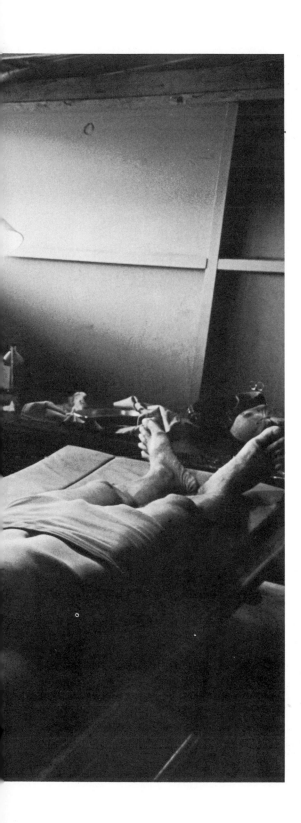

". . . it's rather naive to think that we have any interest in the Vietnamese people. And the government of Vietnam doesn't give a damn about them. They were just caught in the middle of a power struggle."

Dr. Kenneth R. Case, Jr.

It was Sunday afternoon and an aerial weapons company (helicopter gunships) had "volunteered" to fly a group of village children to the beach for the afternoon. The company Public Information Officer made sure the story was released. It was good publicity with Vietnamization going great guns and all.

One of the warrant officers was putting on his helmet and checking his flak jacket when he mused, "I just don't get it. Today we take the little bastards out to the beach and tomorrow we kill them. Just doesn't make sense."

He was a young lieutenant with a Master's degree in agricultural development, and field experience in Central America, the Philippines, and Cambodia before he was "drafted" and given a commission. His first assignment in Vietnam was with a civil affairs company, but he quarreled with the higher-ups over their callous attitude toward the civilian population. One day he just moved out of his office in Da Nang and went across the river to a cubicle in the USAID building. There he put in eighteen-hour days, working on a mammoth report that, if implemented, would improve the economic structure of the Vietnamese living in the region and give them an opportunity to export pork to the south for rice.

When I talked with a colonel who was in charge of much of the civil affairs work, I mentioned I had spent some time with this lieutenant.

"Yes, he's involved in an ambitious work," said the colonel. "His love for these people is really something." Then he added, "You know, I'm amazed at the fine line between him and the kids who are in jail."

Very few GIs are able to know the Vietnamese people as human beings rather than gooks, slopes, or dinks. Most cities and populated areas are off limits, so the GI hasn't the opportunity to meet the people even if he wants to. His only mingling with the people is when he manages to sneak into Saigon or Da Nang or wrangle official permission to spend a few days in the city. And in the cities around American bases the GIs see the cesspool of Vietnamese life.

The comment of a kid on a three-day in-country R & R at Vung Tau is typical: "Boy, did I beat the shit out of a whore. It was really fun. They really have some whore sluts around here. Their women can't fuck, their men can't fight, and their flag speaks for itself—red and yellow."

Saigon—Paris of the Orient

Saigon—"the Paris of the Orient," "the Pearl of the East." When you get there, you find it's now an incredibly jammed city of over three million people, many of them forced off their farms to become refugees.

Saigon is where many GIs get their opinion of the Vietnamese people, and the consensus is always the same—the Vietnamese are whores, beggars, and thieves. The beggars curse the Americans, the bar girls hustle "Saigon tea" at over two bucks a drink and then jeer at the soldiers when they refuse to buy more, and the thieves are legendary. Teen-agers on Hondas can grab a camera or watch without shifting gears or slowing down.

An added problem is the ever growing anti-American feeling in Saigon. Lone drunk GIs are targets for roving bands of Vietnamese who may try to castrate the unfortunate soldier. Armed Forces radio in Saigon carries a commercial that warns, "You came to Vietnam to fight the Viet Cong, not your allies. . . . If you must be out at night, travel in pairs. . . . And never stay out after curfew."

But if the Americans see the worst side of Vietnam in Saigon, it's a good guess that among the thousands of Americans who inhabit the capital, the Vietnamese see the worst side of America.

"Hey, GI, come here. You want young girl? I get
for you. Very nice. You want hash? I get hash for
you. Hey, come here, GI. Fuck you, GI."

BEWARE THE YOUNG GIRLS
SelliNG PEANUTS.

THEY ARE THE
RiCHEST PiCKPOCKETS
IN TOWN !!

"The Mayor of Saigon has requested USAHAC authorities to pass this word to U.S. military men residing in BOQ's and BEQ's in the greater Saigon area. Ask your maid, laundress, or hotel supervisor to keep your uniforms out of sight from the street while they are drying. Use of a clothesline away from the front of the building could be the start toward a better-looking Saigon."

*Military commercial,
broadcast on Armed Forces
Vietnam Network*

The only thing I feel when I kill a gook is the recoil from my M-16.
　　Written in "Guest Book" at the Red Cross building
　　　　　　　　　　at Freedom Hill—DaNang

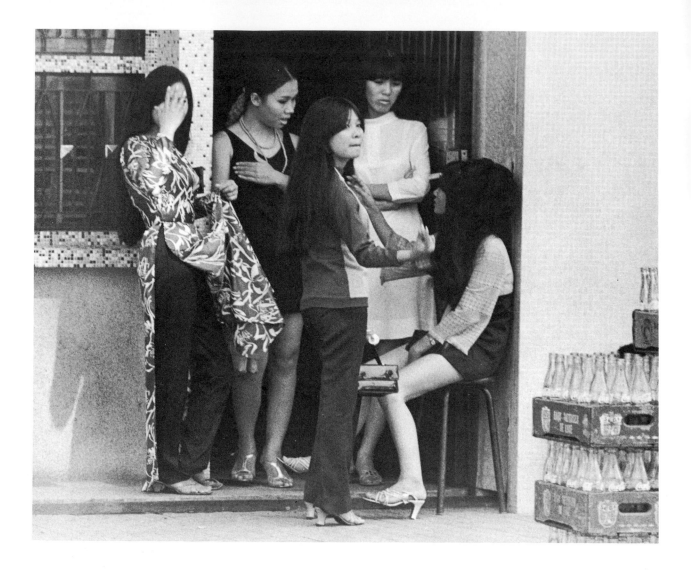

Strains of Bobby Vinton, "Home . . . I'm comin' home."

Announcer: "Do you want to go home? Sure you do. So do I. Well, casualties inflicted by the enemy will be the first thing to stop you. Do you know VD is the second? Avoiding the source is the most ideal way, but I know some of you won't listen to that. The only other way is immediate medical attention. If you're worried, see your medic."

Music: "I'm comin' home . . . I'm comin' home . . ."
Military commercial,
broadcast on Armed Forces
Vietnam Network

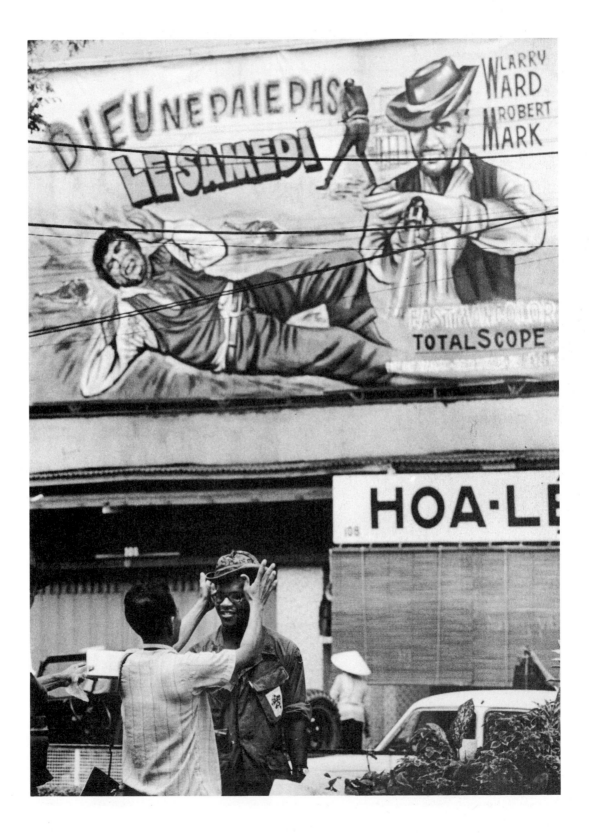

131

134

Once the Americans are past the MPs who stand guard outside the Saigon USO, the desperate whores, the beggars without limbs, and the bloated dying children are shut out. Inside they can enjoy milk shakes and cheeseburgers and watch the skits and shows.

But outside the U.S. enclaves, the up-
heaval continues, as it will for many
years. I'm sure that this man and little
girl are still on the streets of Saigon.
  The man was passive, like most of the
beggars, but the child, who was four
or five years old, would scream and
curse all day at the people who didn't
drop coins in the plastic container.

Turning swords into plowshares

The captain came out of fire direction control and spoke to one of the gunners.

"Shit! We'll have to fire twice as much tonight because they're going to be shooting delayed fuse," said the kid.

"Why's that?"

"Because only half of them will go off, so we fire twice as many."

"You're kidding."

"No, he's right," said the captain.

"You mean all those shells just lay around out there for weeks, or months, or years and could possibly go off any time later?"

"That's right," said the captain.

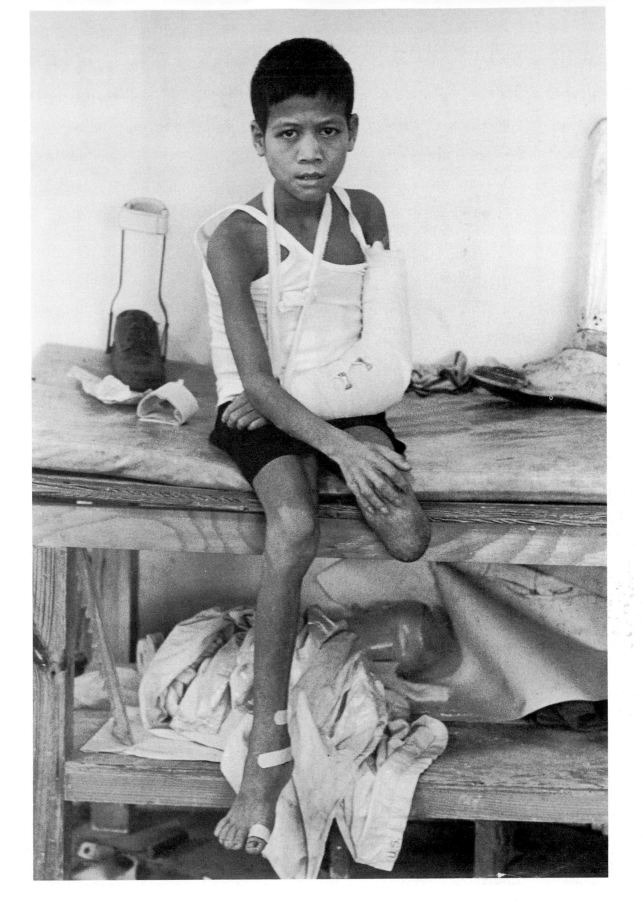

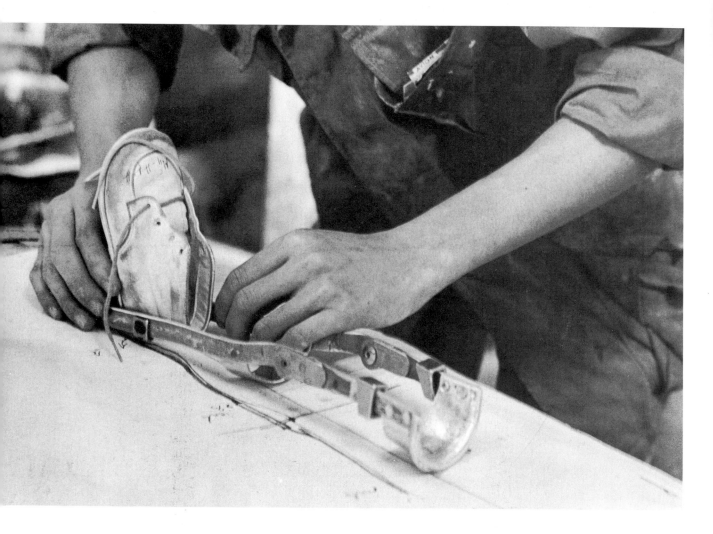

My first glimpse of the real spirit of the Vietnamese people was during a visit to a prosthetics ward in Quang Ngai City. The patients are civilians caught up in the ravages of a war they didn't want and don't understand. About 90 per cent of the injuries are a direct result of warfare and most are attributable to U.S. and South Vietnamese shelling, simply because they expend many times the armament that the North Vietnamese and Viet Cong do. Harassment and interdiction fire (indiscriminate artillery shelling at night to keep roving bands of VC off balance) as well as mines account for many of the injuries. One man in the ward was plowing when a mine went off, killing his water buffalo and taking his leg. A little girl picking flowers later awoke with one arm.

The Center is officially the Quaker Prosthetics Center, sponsored by the American Friends Service Committee, and located within the compound of the Quang Ngai province hospital. The Center is "permitted" to exist by the South Vietnamese government (even though AFSC has sent medical supplies to North Vietnam). "The U.S. government has absolutely nothing to do with the Center," emphasize the workers.

An international staff of young doctors, nurses, physical therapists, and prostheticists run the Center and fabricate artificial limbs without charge for any amputee who presents himself. In addition, they train Vietnamese how to fashion and fit artificial limbs.

"Our methods are sometimes less sophisticated than would be seen in the States, but equally effective," said one doctor. "Lately we've been using Plexiglas from the windshield of a wrecked helicopter to make limbs. Sort of turning swords into plowshares."

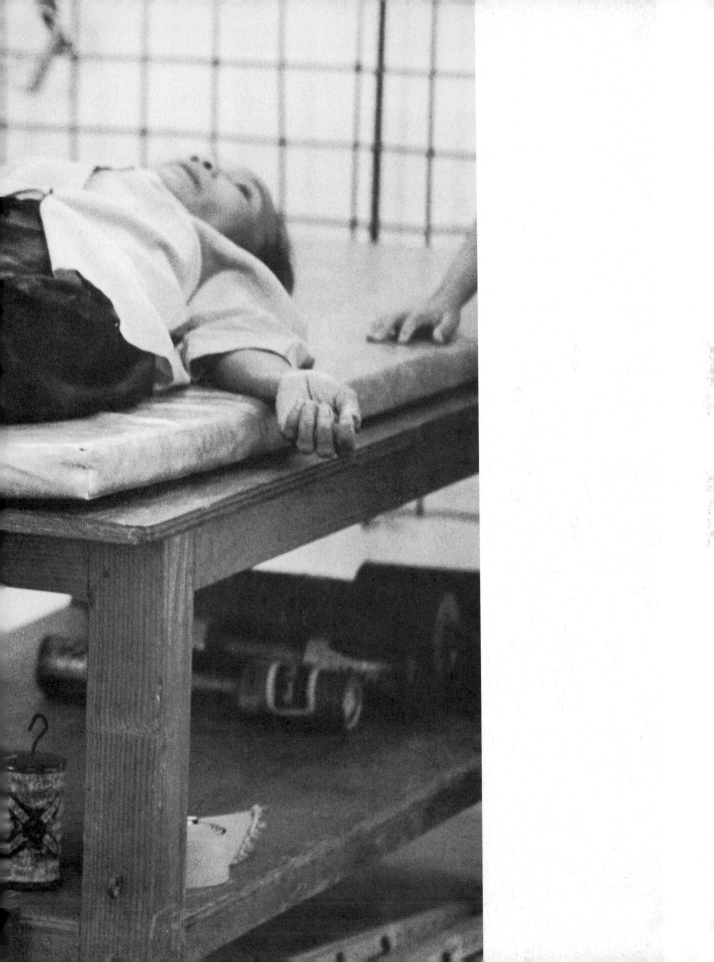

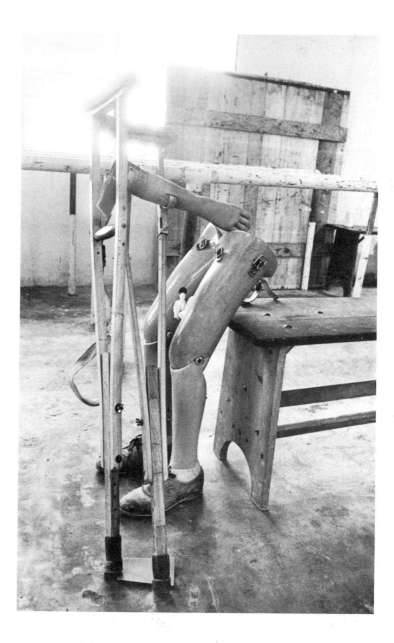

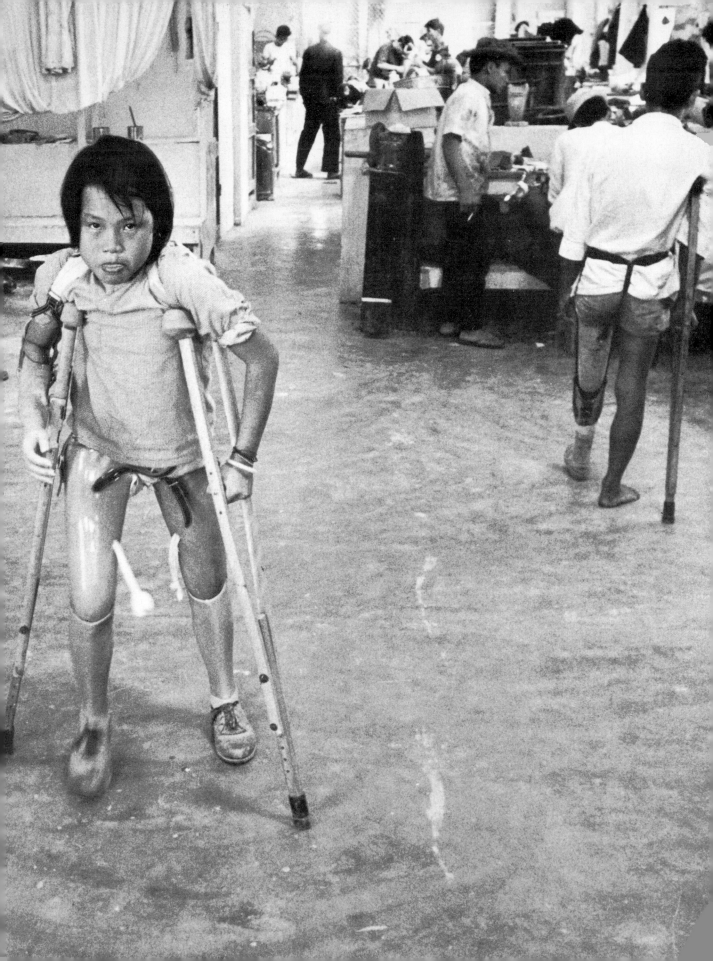

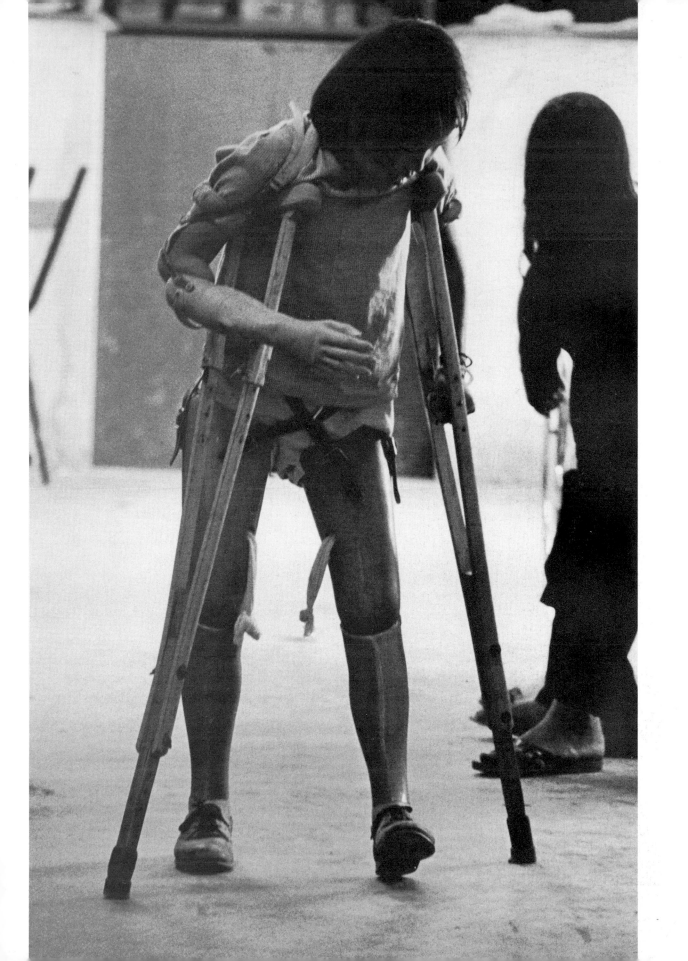

I was reloading my cameras when I noticed a small boy with both legs amputated, smiling at me. I smiled back and said, "Hi," and he shuffled over to my feet. He watched me load one of the cameras. Then he snatched a fresh roll of film from the table and carefully tore off the protective wrapper, shook the cassette out, extended the leader and handed it to me, smiling broadly. In broken English he asked me questions about the cameras—Where they were built? How much the cameras cost?

The AFSC prostheticist walked by and the boy jumped into his arms.

"He's a jolly fellow," I remarked.

"Yes," said the AFSC worker, "his name is Kien. He lives on the porch." He pointed to a section of the porch with mats, a clothesline, some boxes, cans, and jars. "He lives there and entertains his friends by making tea."

"Wow, what an industrious little fellow. How did it happen?"

"He stepped on an American mine which killed his mother and blew off his legs. And his father was killed when the Koreans came into the village firing wildly. At first, one leg was amputated above the knee and the other below, but later both legs had to be done above the knee."

Kien had been listening intently, and the worker gently asked him about what had happened. Kien responded in Vietnamese and the only thing I understood was "mine."

Then Kien suddenly looked at me and blurted out—with too much bitterness for a child—"You no-good GI!" and buried his head in the worker's shoulder.

About the Author

MARK JURY is an author, photographer and filmmaker whose work over the past two decades has often dealt with controversial subjects.

With his brother, Dan Jury, Mark has produced, directed and edited the feature-length documentaries *Dances Sacred and Profane* (1986), which follows an unusual anthropologist on a bizarre trip through American subcults and rituals, and *For All People, For All Time* (1983), which chronicles the fight surrounding the creation of large national recreation areas. "For the Good of All," a one-hour television production on the same subject, was produced, directed and edited by the brothers for the PBS documentary series *Frontline*.

Chillysmith Farm (1981), the first full-length film made by the Jury brothers, was inspired by their best-selling book *Gramp*. This film has received numerous awards, including Blue Ribbon, American Film Festival; CINE Golden Eagle; Best Film, White House Conference on Aging Film Showcase.

Gramp (written with Dan Jury) won the ALA Notable Book Award and the World Understanding Award in the Nikon/University of Missouri competition.

Playtime! America at Leisure was published by Harcourt Brace Jovanovich in 1977.

Mark Jury has had one-person photographic exhibitions at such places as the International Center of Photography, New York City; Soho Photo Gallery, New York City; Ithaca College, Ithaca, New York; Columbia College, Chicago; and Houston Photo Center, Houston, Texas. His photographs have been widely exhibited in group shows, and have been published in books, magazines, anthologies, etc.

The writer/filmmaker lives with his wife, Dee, and their four children in northeastern Pennsylvania.